SENSE OF PLACE

PHOTOGRAPHS OF NEW ZEALAND
ROBIN MORRISON

SAINT
PUBLISHING

CAMEO CINEMA, AUCKLAND

FOREWORD
to the 1999 reprint

Sense of Place was first published in 1984 – fifteen years ago – and was long unavailable until it was reprinted in 1995, and now again in 1999. Robin Morrison, the photographer, died in 1993.

This reprint is timely for two important reasons. Sense of Place was the result of a new direction in Morrison's photography. As well, the images in it retain a potency as strong today as when they were first published.

Sense of Place was Robin Morrison's first retrospective look at New Zealand. Until then most of his photographs had been in black and white: in a twelve-year stretch with the *Listener*, for example, he published over 1000 images, in the form of portraits and photo essays. *Sense of Place* came three years after the critically acclaimed *The South Island of New Zealand – From the Road*. Together they confirmed that the book with colour plates was his favoured medium.

As Robin Morrison wrote in the Foreword, *Sense of Place* is a "collection of visual stories" about how we "present ourselves". In 1999 as in 1984, his images continue to help define what is particular about ourselves and the country we live in.

Peter Hughes

The Robin Morrison Collection is held
at the Auckland Museum

THIS BOOK
is dedicated to my parents,
Ashley and Dorothy

First published 1984
SeTo Publishing Ltd

Reprinted 1995
Saint Publishing Ltd

Reprinted 1997
Saint Publishing Ltd

This reprint 1999
Saint Publishing Ltd

© The Estate of Robin Morrison

ISBN 0-908697-01-5
Designer: Brian Moss
Production: Selwyn Jacobson
Printed in Hong Kong by Colorcraft Ltd

CONTENTS

Front Cover Photograph:
Anglican Church, Raukokore

Back Cover Photograph:
Ross Mitchie, Kaitaia

Photograph on Foreword:
Memorial on Garage, Kaitaia

FOREWORD

Robin Morrison

THE PHOTOGRAPHS IN THIS BOOK form a collection of visual stories concerned with the way we present ourselves as New Zealanders and how we have altered the appearance of this country to reflect our sense of place.

To a certain extent I have documented my own background with these photographs – my ancestors are Scots, English and Irish and I view this country with the eyes of a fifth generation white New Zealander. With this cultural influence the atmosphere in some areas remains foreign to me, especially where the Maori spirit is strong. However, the greatest feeling of alienation comes from repressive and self-righteous attitudes within the white community from people who are unable to shake off the influence of their Puritan forbears.

But for all the alienation that can often be felt, New Zealand still gives me a greater sense of belonging than anywhere else in the world, and I enjoy photographing my country, paradoxes and all.

INTRODUCTION

Peter Ireland

*Eden is a past world in which the contradictions
of the present world have not yet arisen. — W. H. Auden*

THE EUROPEAN CULTURAL DILEMMA in New Zealand was voiced in the use of the word **Home** to describe somewhere else. But although the word has fallen largely from that use, and the dilemma it symbolised less ponderous, the predicament still speaks through the less direct but nonetheless ubiquitous phrase **out here**. **Out here** implies that whatever is considered is considered firstly in terms of somewhere else, and secondly on the understanding that the somewhere else forms a sounder basis for comparison than anything simply **here**. This implication is no longer sustainable. The phrase is out of time and out of place.

It is the fate of a displaced culture that its social and creative dynamisms tend to survive much longer in the new environment than in their place of origin. The stranger and more hostile the new environment the longer they survive. In this way New Zealand often resembles a museum of eighteenth century ideas.

The aesthetic ideas prevailing in Britain at the time of our colonisation were formed essentially in the eighteenth century, arising from that acceleration in European thought known as the Enlightenment, when hope became centred no longer on God but on Science, and in the vacuum of belief Nature became the object of worship and the source of the Ideal. Parallel to prevailing aesthetic ideas was their expression in art, in an idealised style — imbued with a classical harmony having its origins in the previous century in the paintings of Claude — and, as with any style, utilising a range of visual conventions which stressed, in general, ordered composition expressing monumental calm, and, in particular, such method as depicting trees not green but brown. Visual conventions in art relate more to preconceptions of what art should look like, and the values pertaining to the subject matter, than how that subject matter may correspond to the actual physical reality (the portrayal of Christ in Western art for centuries as a model of Greek perfection rather than as the Jew he was is one example). But while visual conventions may be an integral aspect of style — that means whereby experience is made communicable — the danger is, that removed too far in time and space from their origins, they become not expressive but confining factors. A visit to any art society summer exhibition will confirm this. In the eighteenth century nowhere was this dichotomy between the Ideal and the real clearer than in the relationship between art and Nature.

How closely the perfection formerly ascribed to the Deity was now applied to Nature is shown by Sir Joshua

Reynolds' dictum that 'deformity is not nature, but an accidental deviation from her accustomed practice'. And this unblemished Ideal of Nature took its form in the notion of Arcadia. Ovid's factual descriptions of the Greek region of Arcadia as arid and inhospitable were strangely succeeded by Virgil's fantastic vision of a lush pastoral land, inhabited by musical shepherds, untainted by decay. That such a fantasy has for centuries triumphed over fact reveals, perhaps, some need deep in the human psyche for at least the idea of an earthly paradise. And perhaps the need which invented Eden is the same need which seized on the notion of Arcadia in the seventeenth and eighteenth centuries; indeed, the latter replacing the former, as Nature, in a similarly related way, replaced the Deity. In any event, there is a perceptible genealogy from a conception of Eden, through Arcadian ideas, to a notion of God's Own Country.

'Two quite contradictory attitudes to nature', observes Bernard Smith, 'run through much of eighteenth century thought. On the one hand it was claimed that all our misfortunes are due to our departure from nature's laws, while on the other it was claimed that man could only raise himself above the brute creation by improving upon nature.' That precisely states the origins of an unresolved conflict in current attitudes – the anguish on the one hand over Lake Manapouri, and over Aramoana, while on the other the promotion of the **Beautiful New Zealand** campaign, whereby the whole country may yet resemble Hagley Park, that epitome of an eighteenth century improvement upon Nature.

If the demand for paintings with Arcadian themes is an indication, the country most receptive to the idea of Arcadia was England. And this interest was the fertile ground from which sprang a tradition of which we are the unrelenting inheritors; that of landscape painting. A more fateful coincidence of creativity and colonisation could not have been engineered, for, as Nikolaus Pevsner has pointed out, 'the years between just before 1800 and about 1840 saw a prodigious flowering of landscape painting in England, unparalleled in any one country on the Continent'. There seems to be a correlation between the rise of this Arcadian enthusiasm in England and the increasing effects of the Industrial Revolution. The fouler the industrial towns became, the more iniquitous the conditions of labour and housing, the graver rural depopulation and discontent, the more polluted the very air, the more attractive the image of Arcadia became as an intellectual and visual escape.

A physical escape was offered by New Zealand. On this South Sea virgin paradise, it was as if Arcadia actually existed. But what existed was, of course, the old dichotomy between idea and reality: the Ideal may have been unblemished in theory, but Nature in her antipodean particulars proved grimly ungovernable, awesomely untidy, and frighteningly unpredictable. In the face of this, the idea of Arcadia – redundant as an escape from industrial squalor – became a hedge against the overwhelming rawness of colonial New Zealand, and has remained the subterranean cornerstone of our conceptions of worth in art and landscape.

In spite of its apparent realism, photography has embedded within it as many visual conventions as any other expressive medium; indeed, it took on the forms prevailing in painting at the time of its discovery in much the same way as the first motor cars assumed the form of the carriage. And since the history of photography is as old as the national history of New Zealand – the Treaty of Waitangi was signed less than six months after the photographic process had been announced at the Institut de France – the same initially dominant but later restricting visual conventions are common to both. Thus, our decadent tradition of landscape painting and photography that conveys more about eighteenth century notions of composition and preconceptions of art than imparting any biting sense of the real, of what it is like to be alive in the twentieth century. The almost obsessive flow of NZ landscape photo books – those seemingly endless catalogues of standard eighteenth century props of The Beautiful: mountains, lakes, streams, and the bush – tells, in its hardened formula, of a determination to hold on to the idea of Arcadia in the face of the paradoxes and contradictions of our country here and now.

As a fifth generation New Zealander, Robin Morrison both inherits this tradition and reacts against it. He photographs the commonplace uncommonly, transforming the ordinary – what we either fail to see or look at with disdain – into something distinctive, something singularly **ours**. His photographs of the distinctive elements, which together give a location its essential character, convey not only a precise sense of place, but also, collectively, make sense of **this** place. Robin Morrison's work instances, intensifies, and expands our sense of place, not 'out here' but, simply, **here**.

LANDSCAPES

The space, the light and the contrasts of the land are New Zealand's most photographed features. This selection of landscapes eases the eye into the country's physical reality.

GOAT FARM NEAR BROADWOOD

DAWN AT MOUNT PISA

KIDNEY FERNS, RANGITOTO

SNOW IN THE BEECH FOREST, ARTHURS PASS

12

HILLS NEAR CHEVIOT

WANGANUI RIVER, WANGANUI

HILLS NEAR OUTRAM

EVENING IN NORTHLAND, WELLINGTON

ARAMOANA, TOWARDS TAIAROA HEADS

SANDHILLS AT TE PAKI STREAM

ARAMOANA. THE VIEW TOWARDS OTAGO PENINSULA

CLOUD AND WIRES, NEAR MIDDLEMARCH

SUMMER EVENING, NEAR MARTINBOROUGH

MACROCARPA TREE, AUCKLAND

BUILDINGS

New Zealand's European cultural heritage is nowhere better seen than in our architecture. This section of photographs shows the pompous, the homely and the bizarre in our public and private buildings.

There is little tradition in our white culture of blending the architecture from 'home' with the landscape of the new culture, and the resulting warts express a great deal of our feelings towards the land. We have imposed upon it, and the more definite we make our architectural statement, whether through colour or oddness, the more comfortable we seem to be. We are not going to let this country dictate to us how we should build. And if architecture is the mother of art, then the New Zealand landscape is our gallery.

BLUE FARM HOUSE, TANGOIO

FARMERS DEPARTMENT STORE, CHRISTMAS, AUCKLAND

CASTLEPOINT LIGHTHOUSE

STEPS OF THE BAND ROTUNDA, GOVERNMENT GARDENS, ROTORUA

HOUSE IN TAMAKI DRIVE, AUCKLAND

BOXING HALL, WAIPUKURAU

WOMEN'S CENTRE, GREYMOUTH

BANK OF NEW ZEALAND, MIDDLEMARCH

PAKIPAKI RAILWAY STATION, NEAR HASTINGS

COURT OFFICE AND POLICE STATION, MURUPARA

EASTERN VINEYARDS, HENDERSON

DAIRY FACTORY, AWANUI, NEAR KAITAIA

PUBLIC LIBRARY, PUKEKAWA

ECONOMIC STORE, HEREKINO

WHITE HOUSE WITH POODLE, ONGAONGA

BUTCHER'S SHOP, ONGAONGA

YOZIN'S WINERY, SWANSON

MASONIC LODGE, LYTTELTON

BUTCHER'S SHOP OVER THE HOKIANGA, RAWENE

PLUNKET, NGARUAWAHIA

BLUE HOUSE, OTAKI

PINK HOUSE, OAMARU

WOODEN HOUSE, AUCKLAND

RED SHED AND BLACK GOAT, AUCKLAND

FIRE STATION, TOLAGA BAY

BACH WITH TRACTOR AND RED-HOT POKERS, KAIAUA

CHELTENHAM LAVATORIES, AUCKLAND

PEOPLE

Pacific Islanders first settled in New Zealand over one thousand years ago. Less than two hundred years ago Europeans started their domination of the traditional Maori way. However, Maoris, and the later Polynesian settlers, have kept alive much of what is essential to their cultures.

The people in this section are New Zealanders.

BAHAI RECEPTION AT OTAKOU MARAE

GIRL WITH SUNGLASSES AND CHOCOLATE CAKE, OTARA MARKET

COUPLE NEAR OAMARU

DAWN AND CHAPPIE FOLEY, AWANUI

LES NEILSON, BLACKBALL

SHORTY SUTHERLAND, LOWBURN

VILLAGE CRICKET MATCH, PORTOBELLO

PANI TIHORE, TE ARAROA

WOMAN OUTSIDE BUS STATION, DUNEDIN

MAN IN YELLOW T-SHIRT, GISBORNE

HASTINGS A&P SHOW

WALKING THE DOGS, CHRISTCHURCH

LILY SANDILANDS, POSTMISTRESS, TOKIRIMA

ROSS MITCHIE, KAITAIA

FAMILY AT POUTO

IVAN'S RESTAURANT, AUCKLAND

EUROPEAN HOTEL, CHARLESTON

OTAGO CENTRAL HOTEL, HYDE

COLE'S MEALS, TE KUITI

KOSY TEAROOMS, WOODVILLE

PERCY AND PHIL STEED, BUTCHERS, WAIHARARA

MARY AND COTTON McDONALD, CAPE RUNAWAY

MARAEA CAMPBELL ON THE MUSSEL REEF, MITIMITI

TIM JAMIESON'S FRIENDS AND ROSIE, ARAMOANA

VULCAN HOTEL, ST BATHANS

BUCKO ENJOYING A SMOKE AT SUNSET, FOX RIVER

CHURCHES

Early last century missionaries came to this remote colony with an evangelical air and the certainty that their way was best. They taught the word of God as they acquired land for their missions.

Churches were built and many of them still remain, monuments to colonial moral power and the building skills of the pioneers.

CHURCH AT FOX GLACIER. SUMMER TIME

ANGLICAN CHURCH, RAUKOKORE

RATANA CHURCH, TE HAPUA

RATANA CHURCH, RAETIHI

RATANA CONGREGATION, TE KAO

RATANA CHURCH, TE KAO

HIGHER THOUGHT TEMPLE, AUCKLAND

PLASTERBOARD CHURCH AND DANDELIONS, AHIPARA

FIBROLITE CHURCH, RAUKOKORE

CATHOLIC CHURCH, WAIHAU

BRICK CHURCH, MATAKOHE

CHURCH WITH TWO DOGS, NELSON CREEK

CHURCH WITH DOG, KAEO

JESUS HOUSE, AHIPARA

DRAMATIC CHURCH, TUPAROA

BACKYARDS, CARAVANS AND OTHER STRUCTURES

I have found a great deal of pleasure in photographing other people's backyards. The stamp of the owner's personality is more clearly seen in the way they order the side of their lives away from the street view. Caravans, too, have a similar interest for me – colour and oddities in the landscape.

BACKYARD AT LAKE FERRY

CARAVAN UNDER A VERANDAH, CANTERBURY PLAINS

DECORATED PLANTER, KAITAIA

CORRUGATED IRON AND RHUBARB, PORT ALBERT

GERALD AND GERALDINE DE VRIES, ROTOWARO,

PINK BACKYARD, RANGITOTO

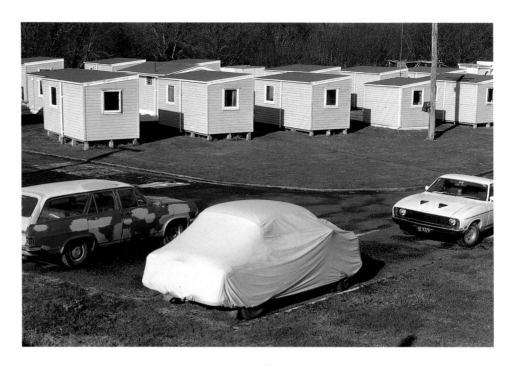

CARS AND HUTS, KING COUNTRY

BLUE CARAVAN AND BACH, TOKAANU

CARAVAN AND BACH, TE HAPUA

GREY BUS AND BACH, TOKAANU

BACKYARD AND WATER TANK, RANGITOTO

CARAVAN BEHIND TREE, LAKE FERRY

DOG KENNEL, MUTTONTOWN GULLY

BACK PORCH, POUTO, KAIPARA HARBOUR

CHILDREN'S PLAYGROUND, DANNEVIRKE

CHILDREN'S PLAYGROUND, QUEENSTOWN

BACKYARD AT PIRINOA

BACKYARD WITH BASKETBALL HOOP, MIRANDA

94

SNOW WHITE, BLUFF

MEMORIALS

In a country that had more casualties per capita in the two world wars of this century than did Britain, it is not surprising that memorials to our losses are found in every corner of New Zealand. Tens of thousands of young men sought adventure overseas. Most went willingly to fight the foe in the Middle East and Europe, and many died in the squalor of France and Belgium not really knowing what it was all about other than that mother England had called them to arms.

Memorials are for the living – a reminder that it wasn't us who died for 'freedom and democracy'. There are no memorials to the equally brave who refused to fight. They also suffered for the notion of freedom.

BILLIARD ROOM AT THE COMBINED SERVICES CLUB, MASTERTON,

SAVAGE MEMORIAL, AUCKLAND

MEMORIAL GATE, PICTON

MEMORIAL GATE, TOLAGA BAY

RSA CLUB, TE AROHA

GLORIT MEMORIAL HALL, KAIPARA HARBOUR

DISAPPEARING GUN ON NORTH HEAD, AUCKLAND

WAR MEMORIAL BATHS, MILLERS FLAT

MEMORIAL TO WORLD WAR 1, OHAKUNE

MEMORIAL GATE IN QUEENSTOWN

HOKIANGA ARCH OF REMEMBRANCE, KOHUKOHU

MEMORIAL AT MOUNT MAUNGANUI

MEMORIAL FLAGPOLE AND SEATS, MATAKOHE

STATUE OF SOLDIER, GOVERNMENT GARDENS, ROTORUA

MEMORIAL GATE, LITTLE RIVER

MEMORIAL GATE, PORT ALBERT

AUCKLAND WAR MEMORIAL MUSEUM

"TO THE GLORIOUS DEAD" AUCKLAND WAR MEMORIAL

ROBIN MORRISON

NEW ZEALAND PUBLICATIONS

IMAGES OF A HOUSE – Robin Morrison, *Alister Taylor*, 1978.

THE SOUTH ISLAND OF NEW ZEALAND: FROM THE ROAD – Robin Morrison, *Alister Taylor*, 1981.

WINES AND VINEYARDS OF NEW ZEALAND – Michael Cooper, Robin Morrison, *Hodder and Stoughton*, 1984 (1st ed.) 1988 (2nd ed.) 1993 (3rd ed.).

SENSE OF PLACE – Robin Morrison, *Seto Publishing*, 1984.

FERNS OF NEW ZEALAND – Susan Firth, Martyn Firth and Elizabeth Firth, Robin Morrison, *Hodder and Stoughton*, 1986 (reprinted 1994).

AUCKLAND: CITY AND SEA – Robin Morrison, *Century Hutchinson*, 1989.

HOME PLACES – Keri Hulme, Robin Morrison, *Hodder and Stoughton*, 1989.

A LAND APART, THE CHATHAM ISLANDS OF NEW ZEALAND – Michael King, Robin Morrison, *Random House*, 1990 (reprinted 1993).

NEW ZEALAND ARCHITECTURE – Peter Shaw, Robin Morrison, *Hodder and Stoughton*, 1991.

AT HOME AND ABROAD – Robin Morrison, *Tandem Press*, 1991 (reprinted 1995).

THE COROMANDEL – Michael King, Robin Morrison, *Tandem Press*, 1993.

A JOURNEY – Robin Morrison, *Tandem Press*, 1994.

PUBLIC COLLECTIONS

Auckland City Art Gallery

National Art Gallery, Wellington

Manawatu Art Gallery, Palmerston North

Robert McDougall Art Gallery, Christchurch

Metropolitan Museum of Art, New York

Waikato Art Museum, Hamilton